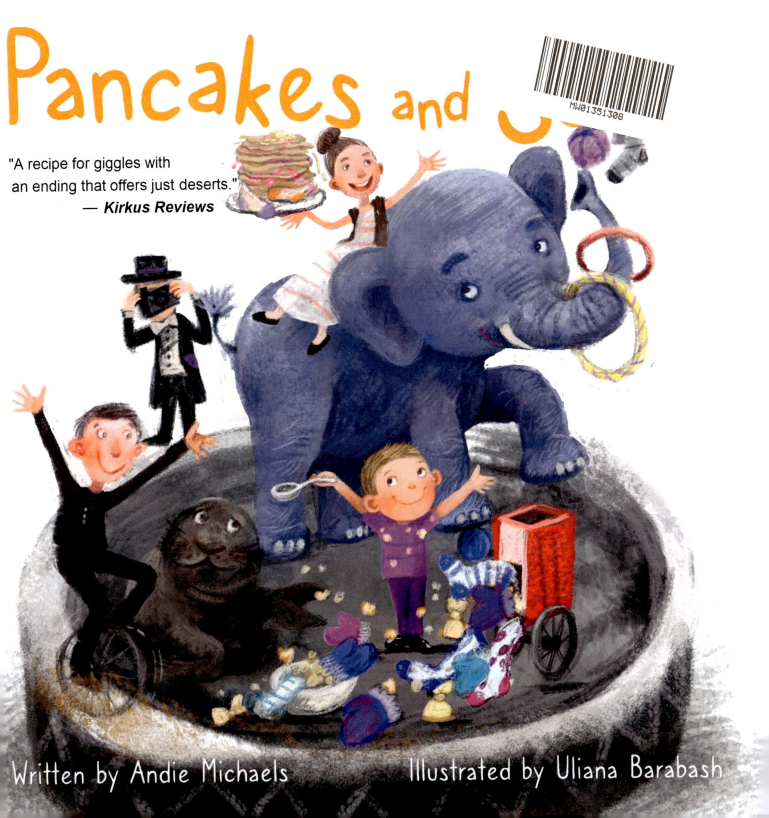

Mulberry Street Publishing, Orange County, CA.

This book, or parts thereof, may not be reproduced in any form without permission in writing from the author, Andie Michaels.

Library of Congress Control Number: 2021904486
Michaels, Andie
Pancakes and Socks / by Andie Michaels ; illustrations by Uliana Barabash

Summary: When a little boy grows tired of the same boring breakfast he decides to cook up his own peculiar fiber-filled creations for his family, turning his house upside down. PANCAKES AND SOCKS is a recipe for silliness, sure to tickle the hearts of children ages 3-7.

ISBN: 978-1-7330663-3-4 (hardcover)
ISBN: 978-1-7330663-7-2 (paperback)

[1. Humor– Juvenile Fiction, 2. Stories that rhyme- Juvenile Fiction – 3. Poetry for early learning.]

Copyright © 2021 Andie Michaels. All rights reserved.
First Edition: July 31, 2021

10 9 8 7 6 5 4 3 2 1

Andie Michaels   www.andiemichaels.com

Sign up for my email list to receive the latest news and free downloads

Printed and bound in the USA

Pancakes and Socks

Written by Andie Michaels

Illustrated by Uliana Barabash

Mulberry Street Publishing, Orange County, CA.

Mom calls us for breakfast.
It's always the same.
The oatmeal is clumpy. It's lumpy and lame.

I *mumble* and *grumble.*

"I'd rather eat thread."

Then

CLICK!

goes a light bulb right over my head.

I grin at my sisters, "I have a surprise!
I'm making your breakfast." They both roll their eyes.

It isn't the usual, I have arranged.

So throw out that GOOP

cause the menu has changed!

Instead of plain cereal, burnt toast and jam,
today we have warm fuzzy earmuffs and yam.
Not hashbrowns and waffles, not bagels and lox,
this morning I'm making peach Pancakes and Socks

I load up a spoon singing, "Here comes the plane!"
Then "Here comes the birdie!" and "Here comes the train!"
Mom said we need fiber, there's fiber in clothes.
This bite goes to Rae then a nibble to Rose.

They **smack** back the spoon,

"Just a smidgen." I cry "one piece of pajamas and peppers on rye."

They squinch, squirm and squiggle they slip side to side.

I grin, "I'll make French toasted tutus, deep-fried!"

I whistle for Pickles.

I'm feeding him too.

Today he'll have slippers in left over stew.

I'll sprinkle the fish bowl with flakes and small ties,

then outside I'll toss some suspenders and fries.

meow Cries Camille and her crate full of kittens.

I'll bring them sardines, macaroni and mittens.

The chipmunks and rabbits will all want to try

my steamed cream of carrot and baseball cap pie.

I'll start my own business; I'll open a stand.
My fiber-filled breakfasts will be in demand.
Just pack up your laundry and bring it to me
I'll sort it, and cook up a ratatouille.

The line will be long, but they'll all want to wait.
Miss Jeepers tells old Mr. Peppers *"It's great!"*
I'll also deliver the meals served in bed,
soy sauce over swim suits, fried eggs over bread.

We'll eat on the terrace;
	first, cheese stuffed in shirts.

Then syrup on roasted Hawaiian grass skirts.

A big bowl of sneakers each soaking in milk
and breakfast burritos in scarves made of silk.

JACK HENRY!

Mom hollers, "This place is a mess!"
She teeters and totters,
YOU BAKED MY NEW DRESS!

My father says, "What in the world have you done?
Go straight to your room I suggest that you run"
I've nothing to wear. I have milk in my shoes.
My face may appear on the 5 o'clock news.

The headlines will read,
"See the kid who eats clothes
Under the Big Top in traveling shows."

Lunch time! calls Mom.

"It's lasagna and lamb,

sauteed with your autographed baseball cards."
BAM!

More books by the author:

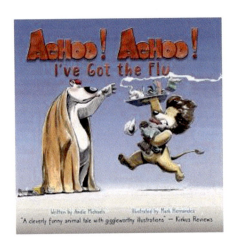

ACHOO! ACHOO! I've Got the Flu

"A cleverly funny animal tale with giggleworthy illustrations."

— *Kirkus Reviews*

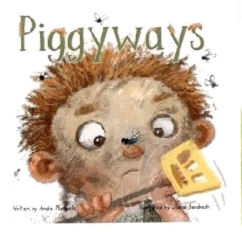

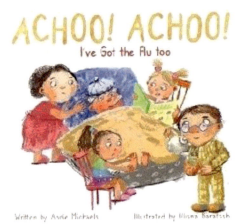

signed copies available when purchased directly from the author at   www.andiemichaels.com

ANDIE MICHAELS is a hair and makeup artist, a black belt in kempo karate and a writer who enjoys telling stories in rhyme. She loves laughing with her family, cooking with her husband, and going for long walks.

Having her picture books published has been a long time dream of hers.

Coming soon...
Mulberry Trio, Three Books in One

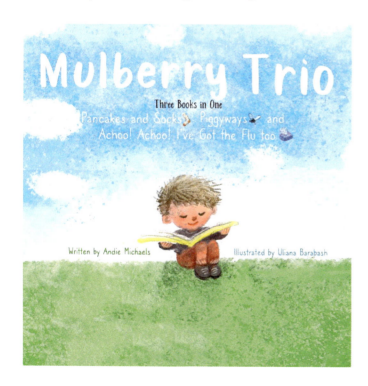

Pancakes and Socks magnets.

Sold exclusively on my website while supplies last.

order soon.

approx 4 1/2" x 3 1/4"   approx 3 1/2" x 3"

get the lastest on new book releases and discounts when you sign up for my email list.

www.andiemichaels.com

Made in the USA
Middletown, DE
29 November 2022